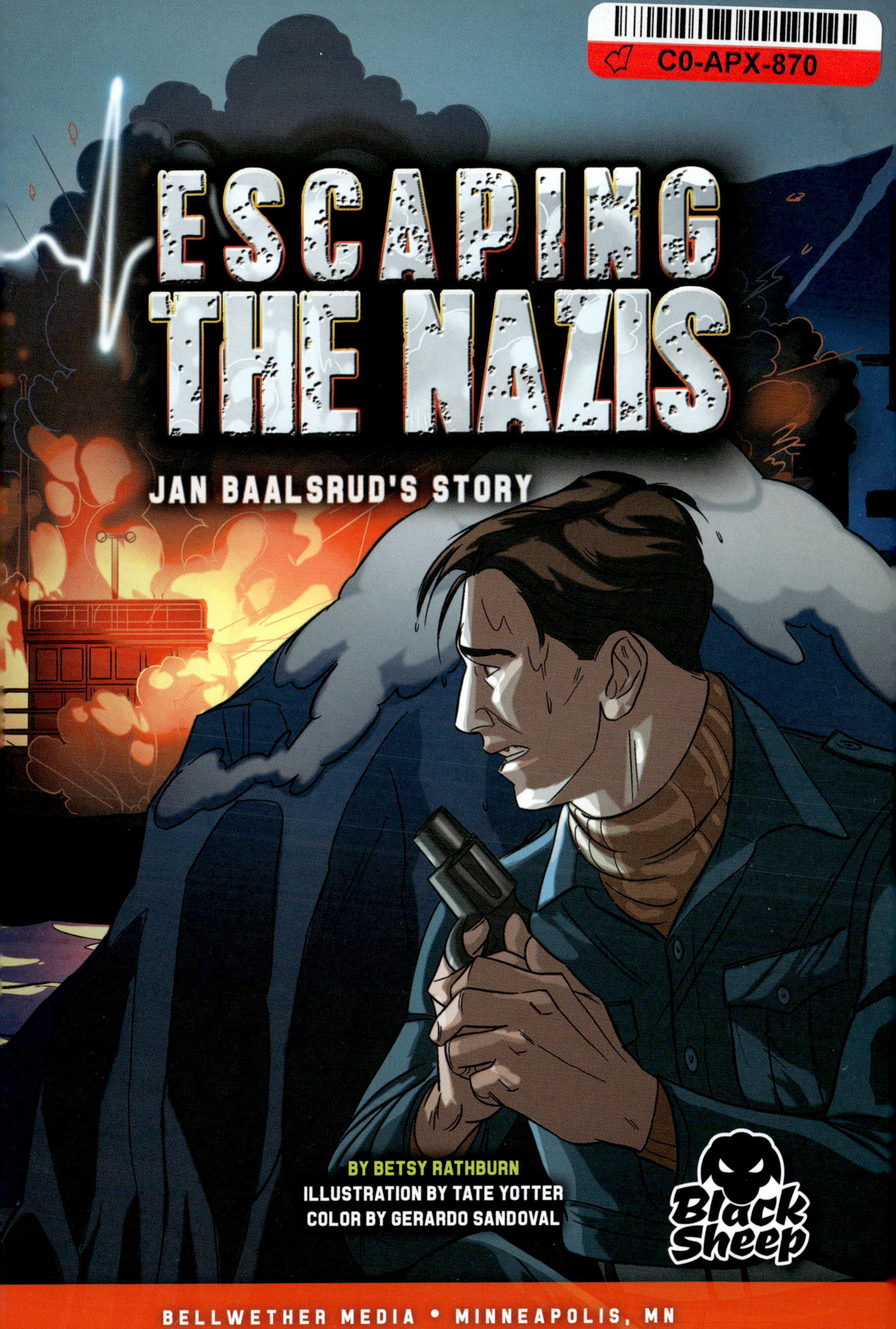

ESCAPING THE NAZIS

JAN BAALSRUD'S STORY

BY BETSY RATHBURN
ILLUSTRATION BY TATE YOTTER
COLOR BY GERARDO SANDOVAL

Black Sheep

BELLWETHER MEDIA • MINNEAPOLIS, MN

This edition first published in 2022 by Bellwether Media, Inc.

Library of Congress Cataloging-in-Publication Data

LC record for Escaping the Nazis: Jan Baalsrud's Story available at https://lccn.loc.gov/2021025030

Editor: Christina Leaf Designer: Andrea Schneider

Printed in the United States of America, North Mankato, MN.

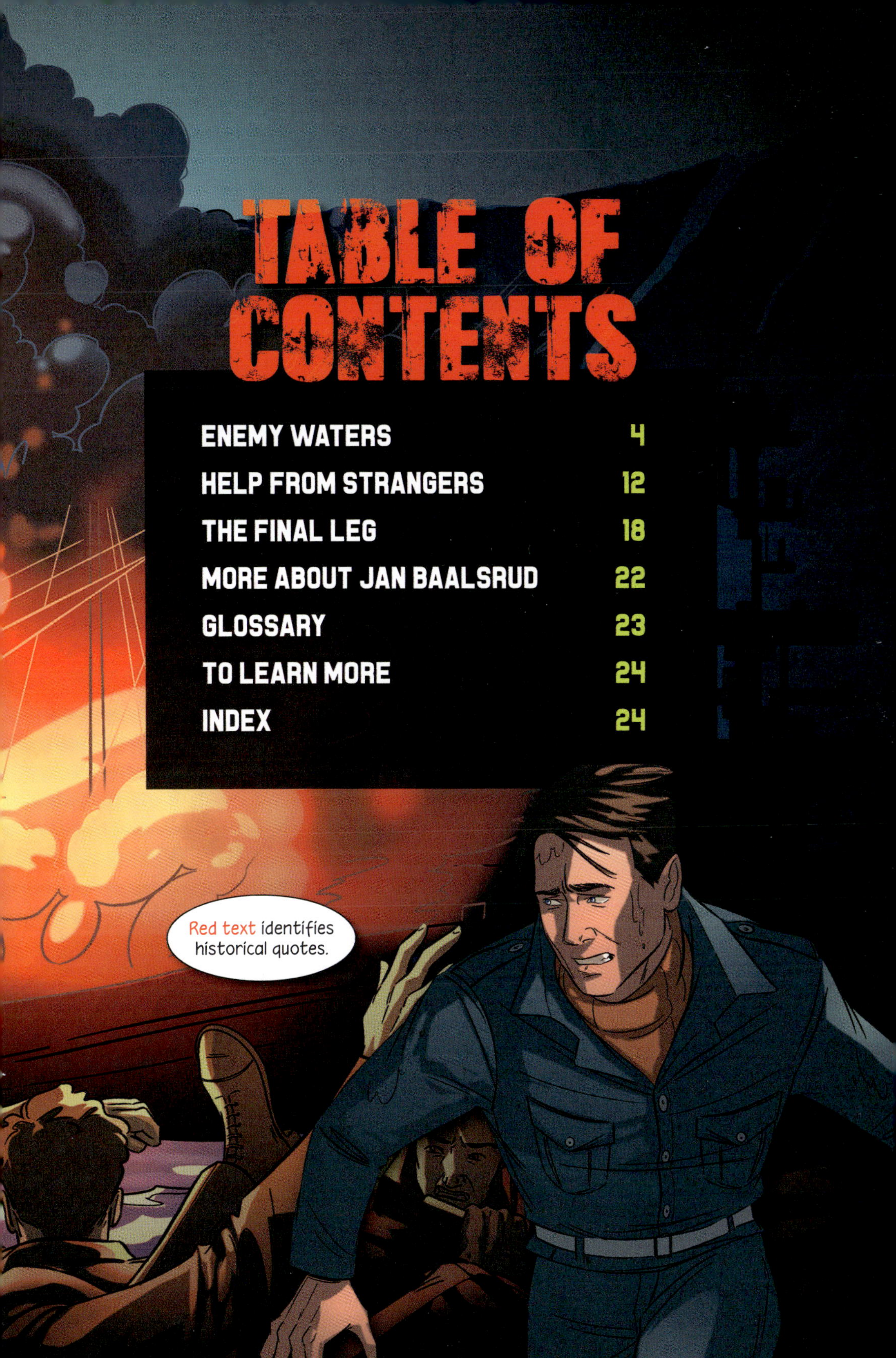

TABLE OF CONTENTS

ENEMY WATERS
March 29, 1943
The *Brattholm* has finally reached its destination. After sailing across the icy Atlantic Ocean for six days, the 12 men on board have arrived in northern Norway. Now, they float in enemy waters.
It feels good to see home.
I only wish this war was over, and we could stay for good.
This mission will help, I hope.
Jan Baalsrud and Per Blindheim are Norwegian soldiers. They left their families to fight in World War II. After training in Scotland, they are back in Norway for the first time since the Nazi **occupation** began.
It looks like things are clear. Let's go down and go over the plan. The others can keep watch.
Yes, Lieutenant Eskeland.
Disguised as a fishing boat, the *Brattholm* has so far gone unnoticed by people on shore. The soldiers on board hope to keep it that way. Their mission is to **sabotage** the Nazi soldiers.

Remember, the Nazis can't learn about our plans. If it looks like they've got us, we'll burn the papers and light one of these fuses.
The *Brattholm* carries many explosives. It also holds top-secret papers. The **resistance** will be in trouble if the papers fall into the wrong hands.
The green fuse lasts 5 minutes. It'll give you time to escape. The blue one lasts 30 seconds, and the red will blow right away. Let's hope it doesn't come to that.
We'll do what we have to do.
Good. Now, try to get some sleep. We'll want to be rested for our trip to Tromsø.
Tromsø is an important Norwegian port city. There, the soldiers' work will begin.

March 30:
As the soldiers rest below deck, the crew keeps watch for enemy ships.
What's that?
Germans! The Germans are here!
Everyone springs into action. But with the Germans approaching fast, the men have no choice. They must abandon the *Brattholm*.
I lit the fuse!
Abandon ship! Abandon ship!

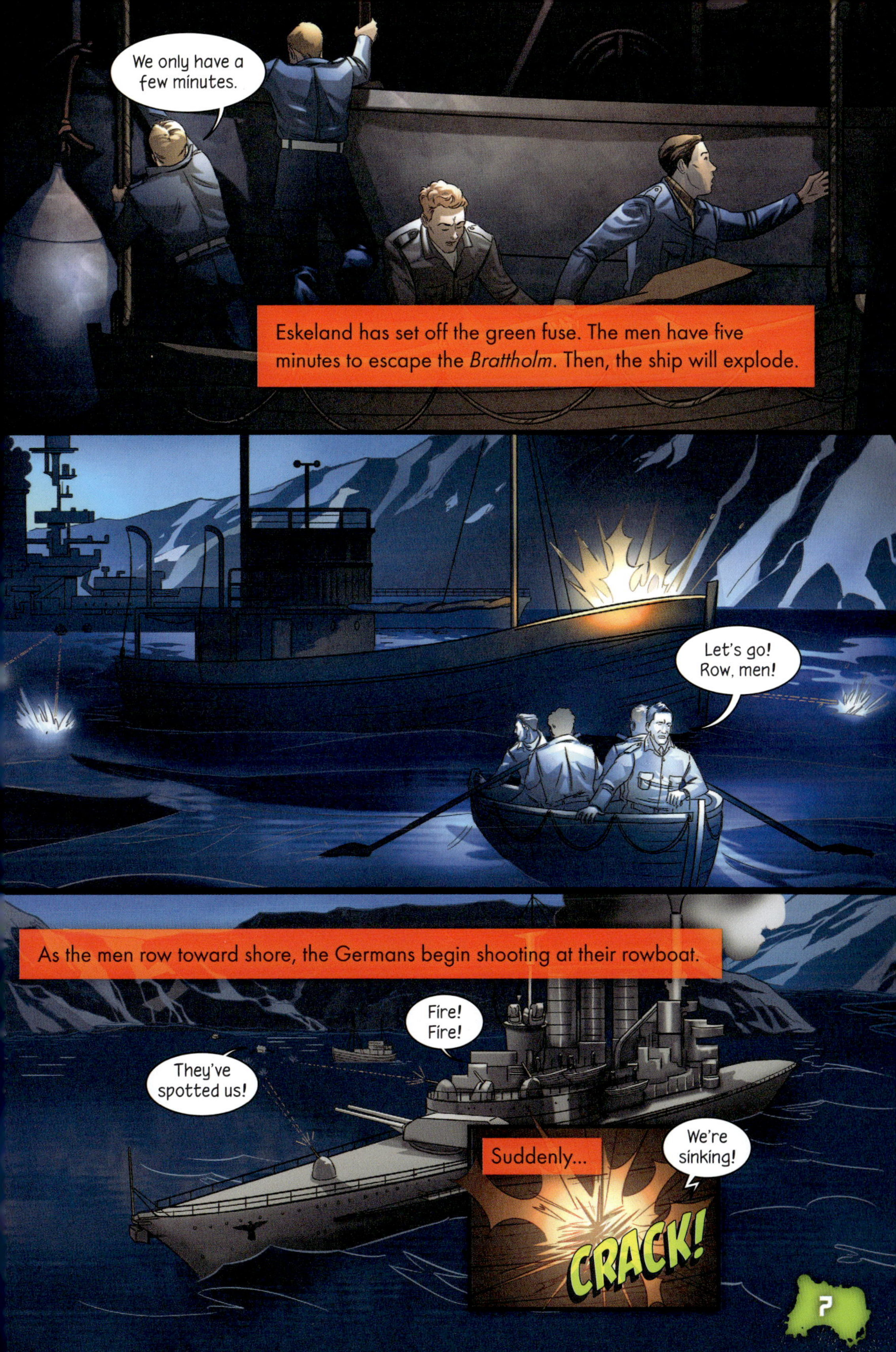
We only have a few minutes.
Eskeland has set off the green fuse. The men have five minutes to escape the *Brattholm*. Then, the ship will explode.
Let's go! Row, men!
As the men row toward shore, the Germans begin shooting at their rowboat.
Fire! Fire!
They've spotted us!
Suddenly...
We're sinking!
CRACK!

But soon after their rowboat is hit...
BOOM!
The force of the explosion knocks Eskeland out of the rowboat. Jan reaches to pull him back onto the boat.
That was a close one. You almost—
BANG!
Another gunshot splinters the sinking rowboat. The soldiers plunge into the freezing water, forced to swim for their lives.

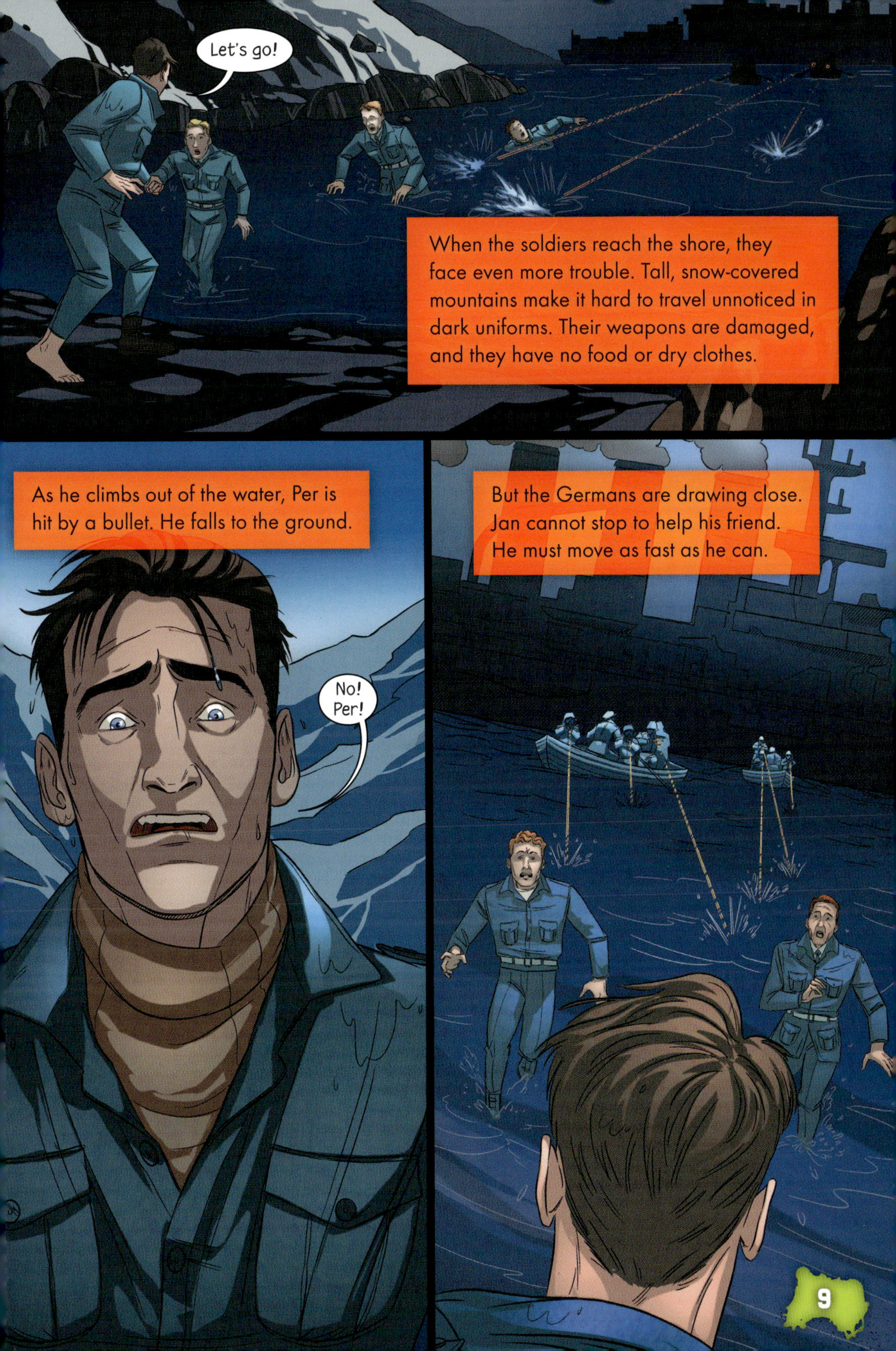
Let's go!
When the soldiers reach the shore, they face even more trouble. Tall, snow-covered mountains make it hard to travel unnoticed in dark uniforms. Their weapons are damaged, and they have no food or dry clothes.
As he climbs out of the water, Per is hit by a bullet. He falls to the ground.
No! Per!
But the Germans are drawing close. Jan cannot stop to help his friend. He must move as fast as he can.

As he climbs away from the shore, Jan is spotted by a Nazi **Gestapo** officer.
You there! Halt!
Surrender at once!
Jan thinks fast. If he is caught, the Nazis could force him to reveal important secrets. He pulls out a gun he had hidden in his coat.
When they come closer, I'll shoot.

CLICK!
Jan pulls the trigger, but nothing happens. Water from the swim has frozen inside the gun. He tries again and again.
BANG! BANG!
Finally, the gun fires. The Gestapo officer and another soldier are hit, and the others run away. Jan is left alone.
Jan makes it to the top of the slope, struggling through deep snow. By now, his wet clothes have frozen solid, and he has lost a boot. His bare foot is so cold, he doesn't realize it has been shot at first.
The Germans are looking for me, and the temperature is dropping. I have to find shelter and dry clothes, and fast. If I don't, I'm as good as dead.

HELP FROM STRANGERS

Jan heads down the mountain and around the edge of the island. He manages to swim a short distance to a small, rocky island. But the Nazis are still on his trail.

My only choice is to swim across. Maybe then, I can find shelter.

He plans to cross more than 600 feet of water, to an island called Hersøya. He noticed a house there earlier. Hopefully, whoever lives there is friendly.

Jan faints when he reaches land. He wakes to two young Norwegian girls standing over him. He does not know how long he was **unconscious**.

The girls lead Jan to their home, where he is quickly welcomed inside. Jan explains his story to the family.
I expect they're still looking for me. I can't stay here.
You must go east to Sweden. They are **neutral**. That's the only way you'll be safe.
I'll row you to the next island, Ringvassøya. There, you can find a man named Jensen.
By now, Jan's clothes are dry, and his foot has been bandaged. He also has a new boot. The journey ahead will be dangerous. But he knows that in Sweden he has a better chance of passing news to his **allies**.
But don't you want me to bring you to Mr. Jensen?
I'll find him myself. Thank you for your help.
When he arrives on the next island, Jan decides to continue on his own. He does not want anyone to know which families helped him. It would be too dangerous.

Jan easily finds the Jensen house...
Is Mr. Jensen home?
No, he left this morning. But won't you come in for breakfast?
...but he soon realizes he cannot stay.
Mr. Jensen will be back in a few days. You must stay here until he returns.
It would be too dangerous for you. I need to keep moving.
Some people here, they can't be trusted. There are Nazis nearby. They'll turn you in!

If I stay here, we're both in danger. I'll leave now, while it's still early. Tell no one you saw me.
Jan will cross the island on his own.
Jan's journey is tough. He must travel across 30 miles of mountainous land. Snowstorms make it almost impossible to see. With every passing moment, the chance of **frostbite** grows.

Jan travels for several days. Deep snow makes his progress slow, but he keeps going.
Along the way, Jan finds help from Norwegian people. Some fear he is a Nazi spy. But once Jan proves he is on their side, they tell him to find Einar Sørensen.
Einar Sørensen and his father, Bernhard, readily help Jan on his journey. They make a plan to cross to the next island by boat.
This weather will help us cross without being seen.
You can use these skis to get to safety quickly. Find a man named Alfred Lockertsen.
Jan quickly finds Lockertsen. The next night, the two set out toward **mainland** Norway in Lockertsen's motorboat.
Germans guard the road, and the mountains are deadly at this time of year. You'll be in great danger.

I have no choice. Thank you for your help, Alfred.
Good luck.
After a week of traveling, Jan has finally made it to the mainland. He is thankful for all the help he has received. He still has many miles to go until he reaches Sweden. But with the new skis, it should be easy to travel quickly.
As he skis, Jan must avoid the Nazi soldiers who patrol the roads. He must also survive the dangers of the Norwegian wilderness.

THE FINAL LEG
Out of the way!
Jan's journey across the Norwegian mainland is filled with danger. On the first day, he speeds through a group of Nazi soldiers. But they do not recognize him.
Later, Jan passes some Nazi soldiers checking ID papers. He has to think fast, or he will be caught. His papers were blown up with the *Brattholm*.
Jan skis past them and climbs high into the mountains to escape.
In the mountains, a strong storm whips up and leaves Jan unable to see. The harsh wind blows snow and ice over him.
Jan creeps slowly along the mountains. But then...

...a sudden **avalanche** sends Jan tumbling down the mountain. He falls for hundreds of feet, rolling over and over.
AHH!
When the avalanche stops, Jan is buried up to his neck in snow.
Luckily, Jan is able to escape the heavy crush of snow. But he now has **snow blindness**. He wanders for three days, dazed.
Then, he stumbles upon the home of Hanna Pedersen. She and her brother, Marius Gronvoll, offer help.
This explains why the Nazis searched us.
They must have been looking for you.
You must tell no one. I'm trying to get to Sweden.
Don't worry. We'll help you.

Marius helps Jan get to Revdal, Norway. There, Jan stays in a small shed for many days. His journey has caused many injuries. Frostbite and **gangrene** in his feet have made it difficult to walk. Jan must rely on others to carry him to Sweden.
How long will you be?
It may be a while. I'll come as soon as I can.
To avoid being found by the Nazis, Marius moves Jan into a hidden cave in the mountains. There, Jan waits for several more days.
Other rescuers bring Jan closer to Sweden. But it is not safe to cross the border yet. Jan must wait in another cave. He lies there for another 17 days.
I don't know if I can go on...

Finally, a group of **Sami** people agree to take Jan into Sweden. But as the border comes into view, Nazi soldiers spot the party.
Go, go!
Halt!
But the Nazis are too far behind. With the help of the Sami, Jan finally reaches Sweden.
Jan spent six months in a Swedish hospital. After losing all of his toes, he had to learn to walk again. Then, he helped train soldiers until the war ended.
Finally, home at last.
Jan returned to Norway after the war. He became a well-known hero for his bravery and determination. But he never forgot the people who helped him escape the Nazis.

MORE ABOUT JAN BAALSRUD

- No one is sure who told the Nazis that the *Brattholm* had arrived. It may have been a shopkeeper who reported it to the Nazis out of fear for his own life.
- Jan was the only survivor of the men aboard the *Brattholm*. The rest were captured and killed or died in the attack.
- Every year, people honor Jan by following his route through the mountains. The celebration lasts eight days.

JAN BAALSRUD'S ROUTE

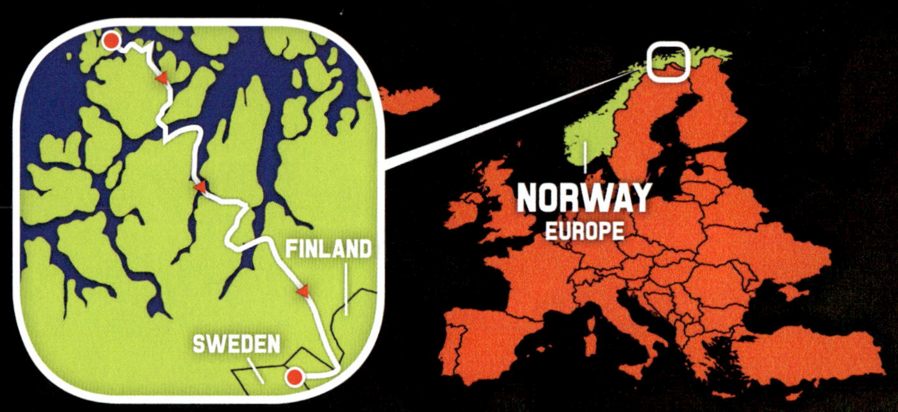

JAN BAALSRUD TIMELINE

March 29, 1943
The *Brattholm* arrives in northern Norway

March 30, 1943
The *Brattholm* explodes

March 31, 1943
Jan is taken to Ringvassøya

April 5, 1943
Jan reaches the mainland of Norway

April 12, 1943
Jan begins his stay in the Revdal cabin

June 1, 1943
Jan reaches Sweden

GLOSSARY

allies—people who work together toward the same goal

avalanche—a sudden event in which a mass of ice, snow, and rock falls down a mountainside

frostbite—damage to the body from being frozen for a long period of time

gangrene—decay in the body caused by a lack of blood supply to the area

Gestapo—the German secret police during World War II

mainland—a continent or main part of a continent

neutral—not aligned with either side

occupation—the holding and controlling of a place by a different country's military

resistance—a group of people who worked to sabotage Germany's actions during World War II

sabotage—to ruin or undermine

Sami—related to the native people of northern Norway, Sweden, Finland, and Russia who are known for herding reindeer

snow blindness—a condition in which someone is temporarily blinded because of snow

surrender—to give oneself up into the power of another person

unconscious—not awake, especially because of an injury

TO LEARN MORE

AT THE LIBRARY

Bowman, Chris. *Norway*. Minneapolis, Minn.: Bellwether Media, 2020.

Burgan, Michael. *Fighting to Survive the Polar Regions: Terrifying True Stories*. North Mankato, Minn.: Compass Point Books, 2020.

Williams, Brian. *World War II*. New York, N.Y.: DK Publishing, 2017.

ON THE WEB

FACTSURFER

Factsurfer.com gives you a safe, fun way to find more information.

1. Go to www.factsurfer.com
2. Enter "Jan Baalsrud" into the search box and click 🔍.
3. Select your book cover to see a list of related content.

INDEX